GEORGIA'S CHARTER OF 1732

EDITED BY
ALBERT B. SAYE
ASSISTANT PROFESSOR OF POLITICAL SCIENCE
THE UNIVERSITY OF GEORGIA

ATHENS
THE UNIVERSITY OF GEORGIA PRESS
1942

The Georgia Open History Library has been made possible in part by a major grant from the National Endowment for the Humanities: Democracy demands wisdom. Any views, findings, conclusions, or recommendations expressed in this collection, do not necessarily represent those of the National Endowment for the Humanities.

NATIONAL
ENDOWMENT
FOR THE
HUMANITIES

Reissue published in 2021

Most University Press titles are available
from popular e-book vendors.

Printed digitally

ISBN 9780820359786 (Hardcover)
ISBN 9780820359793 (Paperback)
ISBN 9780820359779 (Ebook)

Foreword to the Reissue

Georgia was founded as a grand experiment by a group of men with only the best of intentions: to provide new lives for the poor and indigent. The leader of this group, James Edward Oglethorpe, along with William Wilberforce and Granville Sharp, would become early voices for the abolition of slavery in the British Empire. In addition to opening its doors to the poor, the Georgia Experiment also prohibited slavery and rum. This ideological foundation was untenable in a region dominated by a planter aristocracy just across the Savannah River in South Carolina. Though no legislation has been found to prove such, it is also reported that the "scourge" of lawyers was prohibited in the new Georgia colony. This writer is thankful such a prohibition did not prevail.

Albert Saye, the great Georgia historian and political scientist, was an expert on all things Georgia. His imprint on our history and thought is unmistakable. As a lawyer I have used Saye's *A Constitutional History of Georgia, 1732–1945* as a reference for legal research on many occasions. His insight and analysis are thorough and exhaustive. Saye would eventually write twelve books on Georgia history and government. Among Saye's greatest achievements were his three books on Georgia history—each of which served as a textbook for middle schoolers in Georgia for decades. Saye sought to instill in these young students the love of Georgia that burned so brightly within him.

Saye was born in Rutledge, Morgan County, in 1912. He attended Emory University for two years and then transferred to the University of Georgia in 1933, graduating with a degree in history in 1934. Saye received a master's degree at the University of Georgia in 1935. There he became the colleague of Georgia history giants E. Merton Coulter and Kenneth Coleman. After graduating from the University of Georgia, Saye spent a year studying at the University of Dijon in France. He began working on a doctoral dissertation and received his PhD at Harvard University in 1941. The subject of Saye's dissertation was the charter of Georgia.

Though the charter for the Georgia colony—the subject of this pamphlet—had remarkable philosophical underpinnings, it also contained a healthy dose of pragmatism. More than just providing relief for indigents in the London area and acting as a shining beacon of free labor, Georgia also provided a buffer for South Carolina from Spanish Florida. Then, as now, the collision of greed and good intentions proved a powerful force.

Yet some aspects of the Georgia Charter were remarkably progressive. No Trustee could receive land in the new colony or pay for their service as a Trustee. This revolutionary idea was in contrast to the proprietary colonies that granted thousands of acres to their landed gentry. Herbert L. Osgood has observed that the prohibition of private gain by the founders was sufficient to demonstrate "a radical difference between Georgia and all other proprietary provinces" with regard to its founding.[1] The transparent nature of the colony's inner workings was also revolutionary. Meetings and records of the operation of Georgia and expenditures were reported annually. Such was the dream of the Georgia Experiment.

Though laudable, the Georgia Charter had problems in actual administration. The term of the Charter was twenty-one years, hardly the basis of erecting a long-term, stable governance of the colony. No law was final until approved by the king, a long and laborious process that British bureaucracy and transatlantic crossings unduly prolonged. The governor of the colony had to be approved by the king, a process so difficult a governor was never appointed during the Trustee Period. The command of Georgia's militia was placed in the hands of the governor of South Carolina—an insult to the ability of Georgians to defend themselves. And then there were the reports.

The Trustees were required to annually report all receipts and expenditures with any two of the Crown offices, and annual reports were required on each fifty-acre land grant. Governmental red tape is not a modern phenomenon—it seems to have been with us from our beginning.

Sadly, the utopian dream of this special place called Georgia was not to be. Throughout the Trustee Period "malcontents" agitated for more control, freedom from the moralistic strictures imposed by the Trustees, and most important the legal ability to engage slavery. During the Trustee Period, Georgians looked across the Savannah River to see the great wealth brought about by the labor of the enslaved. Despite the inhumanity and immorality of the institution, Georgians wanted the same opportunity at economic success. Georgians were demanding their share of America's original sin. Negotiations began in 1751 to surrender Georgia's Charter, and in 1752 the Crown took control of the colony with all the advantages and ills brought about by such status.

History is full of what ifs. What if the Georgia Experiment had been extended? Would Georgia have joined the other southern states in the Civil War? Probably not. Slavery was the guiding force in the Civil War and with no slaves, the secession movement probably would have foundered. The failed experiment in Georgia could have been a shining example of free people unburdened by greed. Such was not to be.

We are all thankful Albert Saye preserved the history and legacy of the Georgia Experiment with his *Georgia's Charter of 1732*. The University of Georgia Press should be commended for keeping the memory of Dr. Saye alive as well.

ROY E. BARNES

Note

1. Herbert L. Osgood, *The American Colonies in the Eighteenth Century* (New York, 1924), 36–37.

PREFACE

The need for an accurate copy of the Charter of Georgia will become apparent to anyone comparing the printed copies in *The Colonial Records of Georgia*, Macdonald's *Select Charters*, McElreath's *Treatise on the Constitution of Georgia*, and other sources that have been relied upon. There is considerable variation in the order in which the provisions appear in the various copies, and dozens of differences in phraseology. Not one of them gives an accurate list of the members of the Common Council of Trustees. Three dots indicate in some instances the omission of half a page.

The copy presented here is a facsimile of the Charter in the Patent Roll of the British Public Record Office (*Tertia Pars Patentium de Anno Regni Regis Georgii Secundi Quinto*, C.66/3586). In an entry of January 21, 1741, the Board of Trade refers to this copy in the Patent Roll as "an authentic copy . . . that has been collated with the original charter, communicated by Mr. Oglethorpe" (*Journal*, 367). I have been unable to locate the original Charter, even with the cooperation of Dr. Arthur Percival Newton, Editor of the *Calendar of State Papers*. But in any case the copy in the Patent Roll is the preferable one to quote as it would have constituted the official document in case of conflicting provisions. There are several other manuscript copies preserved in the Public Record Office. The copy in C.O.5/670 seems to be the one followed by the Editor of *The Colonial Records of Georgia*. In the Board of Trade's *Entry Book of Commissions, 1740-1781* (C.O.324/49, pp. 81-115), appears a copy which, according to a statement at the end of it, "was examined and compared with the original Charter, received from James Oglethorpe . . . 8th Nov. 1732." This copy was recently printed in the *Calendar of State Papers . . . America and West Indies* (London, 1939), but, regrettably, with a few abridgments.

The Crown officials seem to have had difficulty in transcribing the Charter. June 9th was officially accepted as the date for granting it, but in point of fact, it did not pass the seal until sometime in July. On July 3rd Lord Percival went to take the oath as President of the Georgia Corporation, but, records the entry in his *Diary*, "I learned that some mistakes happening in transcribing the charter, it is necessary they should be amended, and the seal put to it anew. I desired the charter when amended might be sent to my house on Tuesday next."

As I have attempted an interpretative account of the genesis of the Colony of Georgia in two articles appearing in the September and December issues of the *Georgia Historical Quarterly*, 1940, a purely factual account of the steps involved in the granting of the Charter is presented here with a minimum of evaluating comment. This is followed by an analysis of the document.

For assistance in the preparation of this publication I am indebted to two persons in particular, Miss Virginia Bever of the University of California who without charge made the photographs of the Charter from the Patent Roll, and my sister, Mrs. Robert Hillyer Still, who is largely responsible for the tedious task of deciphering the document. The Lewis H. Beck Foundation has given financial support to the publication, and I am grateful to those associated with this Foundation for encouraging my efforts at research in the field of Georgia history.

A. B. S.

Athens, Georgia.
August, 1941.

PART I

INTRODUCTORY STATEMENT

In the two decades preceding the granting of the Charter of Georgia in 1732 some half a dozen attempts were made at establishing a new English colony in America. Projects such as those of Thomas Coram, David Dunbar, William Keith, Robert Montgomery, and Jean Pierre Purry were no doubt instrumental in directing the attention of James Edward Oglethorpe to colonization. The first recorded mention of Oglethorpe's scheme of combining a philanthropic enterprise with the planting of a new colony is found in the entry of the *Diary* of John, Lord Viscount Percival for February 13, 1730.[1] At this early stage the scheme involved the combining of two charity legacies.

A certain haberdasher named King left the sum of £15,000 as a charity legacy "to be disposed of as his executors should please." One of the three trustees into whose hands this sum passed was the heir of the testator and refused to concur with the two others in any method for disposing of the money, "in hopes, as they were seventy years old each of them, they would die soon, and he should remain only surviving trustee, and then might apply it all to his own use."[2] A lawsuit arose out of a proposal to lodge the money in the Mastery of Chancery's hands until new trustees should be appointed. Oglethorpe represented and won the case for the two elderly trustees who then desired that the King fund be annexed to some trusteeship already

---

[1] *Dairy of John Percival, First Earl of Egmont* (Hist. MSS. Reports, 3 vol., London, 1920-23), I, 45-46.

[2] Egmont's *Diary*, I, 90.

existing. For this Oglethorpe suggested the D'Allone charity legacy which was in the hands of four Associates of the late Dr. Thomas Bray, the celebrated philanthropist to whose organizing genius the Society for Promoting Christian Knowledge and the Society for the Propagation of the Gospel in Foreign Parts stand as monuments.

Dr. Bray had encountered and gained the esteem of Mr. Abel Tassin D'Allone, "a gentleman not more celebrated for his penetration and address in state affairs than for a pious disposition of mind," during a visit made to Holland for soliciting the assistance of King William for some of his philanthropic projects. Upon his death D'Allone bequeathed a portion of his English estate to Dr. Bray and his Associates "toward erecting a capital fund or stock for converting Negroes in the British plantations." Dr. Bray was informed by Lord Viscount Palmerston soon after Mr. D'Allone's death with his having left this noble bequest which amounted to £900. "And as it happened that soon after, namely, in Christmas, 1723, Dr. Bray had so dangerous a sickness that his recovery was out of hope, Lord Palmerston was pleased to intimate that it would be requisite he should nominate and appoint, by deed, such as he would desire to have associated with him in the disposition of the legacy. This he accordingly did, choosing gentlemen, of whose affection to this and his other pious designs he had ample experience."[3]

Among the four Associates chosen by Dr. Bray upon whom the D'Allone Fund devolved at the venerable Doctor's death was Viscount Percival, later first Earl of Egmont. Lord Percival was a prominent member of the House of Commons and an influential personage at the Royal Court. Oglethorpe and Percival were friends and had been closely

---

[3] Samuel Smith (?), *Publick Spirit Illustrated in the Life and Designs of the Reverend Thomas Bray.* Published anonymously at London in 1746, this work has been taken as the official biography by the Associates of Dr. Bray. A reprint appeared in 1808.

associated since their joint work on the Parliamentary Committees for investigating the conditions in the English prisons. From the beginning Percival approved of Oglethorpe's proposal to join the two charity legacies as a step toward inaugurating a colonizing enterprise, and soon he began an active collaboration. On April 11th he made a visit to the Temple in connection with legal action for enlarging the D'Allone trusteeship. This process was completed by July 1st, for on that date Percival went to a meeting "of the new Society for fulfilling Mr. D'Allone's will in the conversion of Negroes, and disposing of five thousand pounds, a charity that will be put into our hands by Mr. King's trustees. . . ."[4]

Once this "new Society" had been formed, definite steps were taken toward securing a charter for the enterprise. On July 25, 1730, Oglethorpe dined with Lord Percival and discussed with him questions relative to the charter. Five days later Percival records having attended a meeting where "a petition to the King and Council for obtaining a grant of lands on the southwest of Carolina for settling poor persons of London" was agreed upon. The seven Associates present at this meeting signed the engrossed petition, but it could hardly have been presented to the Privy Council on that date for "the other Associates were to be spoke also to sign it before delivered."[5]

It is probable that this petition was not presented to a meeting of the Privy Council earlier than September 17th.[6]

---

[4] Egmont's *Diary*, I, 98. The two elderly trustees of the King Legacy did not wish for the moment to put more than £5,000 at the disposal of the new trust.

[5] Egmont's *Diary*, I, 99.

[6] W. L. Grant and James Munro, Editors, *Acts of Privy Council, Colonial Series* (London, 1910), III, 299. Among the MSS. of the Marquess Townshend at Raynam Hall, Norfolk, is *An Account of the several steps taken by the Privy Council upon granting the Georgia Charter.* "This account begins with noting the receipt of the Petition of Lord Percival and others on the 17th Sept. 1730, and concludes with stating that the Charter passed the Great Seal on the 9th June, 1732." Hist. MSS. Commission's *Eleventh Report* (1887), Appendix, Part IV, p. 258.

Its provisions were general in character, probably written out during the course of the meeting of the Associates on July 30th, and designed more to start the proposal on its journey through the slowly moving administrative procedure of the day than to be a guide for the specific provisions of a charter. The petition began by pointing to the well known fact that the cities of London and Westminster abounded with "great numbers of indigent persons who were reduced to such necessities as to become burdensome to the publick." These persons, it was declared, would be willing to seek a livelihood in America if only they were provided with passage and the means of settling there. The petitioners, "well assured of considerable contributions," were desirous of promoting this beneficial undertaking. His Majesty was reminded that the great tract of land was unsettled which lay between the Savannah and Altamaha Rivers within the Province of South Carolina which by recent agreement with the former Proprietors had reverted to the Crown. To establish a settlement there would be a great service to his Majesty's Province of South Carolina and in some measure to all the Colonies to which this Province was a southern frontier. The petitioners therefore prayed for a grant of this tract of land, together with a charter of incorporation whereby they should be enabled to enter into contact with such families as were willing to settle thereon, to receive charitable benefaction - from those desirous of promoting the worthy cause, and to make the necessary by-laws for the well-ordering of the intended Colony.[7]

This petition was referred to a Committee of the Privy Council. At this period the Privy Council itself was more of a registering than a deliberating body, its formal meetings being a convenient place for paying compliments to the

---

[7] Arthur Percival Newton, Editor, *Calendar of State Papers, Colonial Series: America and West Indies, 1730* (London, 1930), pp. 357-358.

King, seeing friends, and hearing the latest news. Any business matter of importance was always passed on to a smaller group of four or five members, named interchangeably in the *Acts of the Privy Council*, as "a" or "the" Committee, indicating that there was really but one committee and that it acted somewhat as a committee of the whole. Following a procedure not unusual, this Committee, on November 23rd, in turn referred the Petition here under consideration to the Commissioners for Trade and Plantations, commonly known as the Board of Trade, to "report the properest method to render the same of most service to the public."[8]

On December 3rd, Oglethorpe and three of his former collaborators on the Parliamentary "Committee on the State of the Gaols," Messrs. Towers, Hucks and Heathcote, together with Sir John Gonson, appeared for a hearing before the Board of Trade.[9] As might have been expected in view of the general terms used in the original petition, the Board of Trade was desirous that "these gentlemen would put into writing their particular proposals."

The fact that the *Acts of the Privy Council* record the original Petition as coming from Lord Percival, the Hon. Edward Digby "and others" has led to considerable speculation as to whether Oglethorpe was among the petitioners. He was, of course.[10] In fact, it would be nearer the truth of the matter to think of the petition as having come from "Oglethorpe and others," giving the greater weight to the first term of the addition. This view is supported by the fact that the request of the Board of Trade that the petitioners submit a detailed statement of their proposals was met

[8] *Acts of Privy Council*, III, 300; O. M. Dickerson, *American Colonial Government. 1690-1765* (Cleveland, 1912), pp. 84-100, *passim*.

[9] K. H. Ledward, Editor, *Journal of the Commissioners for Trade and Plantation, 1728-34*, p. 165.

[10] The names of Lord Percival, Edward Digby, and George Carpenter were no doubt placed at the head of the list with the view of securing action upon the petition.

by an unsigned "Memorial" accompanied by a brief statement in the form of a letter from Oglethorpe to Alfred Popple, Secretary to the Board of Trade.[11] It was this Memorial which served as the basis upon which the Charter was drawn up.

The record of the steps intervening between the presentation of this Memorial and the granting of the Charter in its final form is a tedious one of conferences and consultations between the petitioners and the several boards, commissions, and law officers of the British Government. There were hearings and re-hearings before the Board of Trade, meetings of the petitioners with the Committee of the Privy Council, meetings of small groups of those concerned at the Cyder House, Bedford Arms Tavern, the Horn, or, more commonly, at the House of Commons, and many a hint passed to the officers concerned either in private conversation or through their friends. No one officer or board can be blamed for the long delay which elapsed. The fault lay in the loosely organized, and, from the point of view of colonial affairs at least, inefficient administration of the day. More than once there were threats of "flinging up" the affair on the part of disgusted petitioners. As in the early stages, Oglethorpe continued to be the guiding spirit of the group. Lord Percival used his personal influence to advantage on several occasions. But despite the diligent efforts and skillful manoeuvers of Oglethorpe and his coworkers, it took nearly two years to secure the approval of a charter acceptable to all parties concerned. An agreement had to be reached with Lord Carteret, heir of the Carolina Proprietor, who had not relinquished his rights; the Board of Trade had to be convinced that the holdings of the Corporation in "goods and chattels" should not be "stinted;" the clauses inserted by the Attorney General providing for a new election to the Common Council every

[11] *America and West Indies, 1730,* pp. 383-384.

three years, thus tending to "convert the scheme into a job," had to be weeded out. Only the most difficult among these problems is here singled out for a brief consideration: *i. e.*, the relation of the new colony to South Carolina.

Upon this point the Petitioners would not compromise: either the new colony should be set up independent of South Carolina, or it should not be established at all so far as they were concerned. Hence it is that the first report of the Board of Trade, that of December 17, 1730, formulated after two hearings with the Petitioners, stated:

> . . . whereas it is the desire of the Petitioners, that the tract of land petitioned for . . . may be separated from the Province of South Carolina, and be made a Colony independent thereof with respect to their Laws, Government, economy, both civil and military, save only in the command of their militia which is to remain with H. M. Governor of South Carolina for the time being, we are humbly of opinion that H. M. may be graciously pleased to indulge them in this particular likewise, saving always the Dominion of the Crown and the dependence which every British Colony ought to have upon H. M.[12]

In the end the Petitioners succeeded in freeing the new Colony from all control from South Carolina, except in that the chief command of the militia was placed in the Governor of South Carolina, and in that the surveyor of South Carolina was given the right to inspect and survey in Georgia to determine the amounts of quit-rents. It was fear that Georgia would be abandoned as a separate colony and incorporated into South Carolina that led the Trustees in later years to establish the semblance of a legislative body in the Colony.

Even after the Charter was approved by the Privy Council in January 1732,[13] there was still insistence from some quar-

---

[12] *America and West Indies, 1730,* p. 395.
[13] *Acts of Privy Council,* III, 305.

ters on making the new Colony dependent upon South Carolina and this caused a delay of four months. Some blamed this delay upon the Duke of Newcastle, Secretary of State for Colonial Affairs; others declared that it was Walpole who was holding up the Charter; both denied the charge. In reply to certain queries presented in February, Walpole declared that it was not proper for him to tell who was holding up the Charter. His conversations with Percival indicate that the delay was caused by the King. On March 10th, for example, he assured Percival that the objections to the Charter were the King's and not his own. Walpole was astonished to learn that the gentlemen concerned held him responsible for the delay. "There were," he declared, "times when things could be done, other times when they could not, but he would take the proper time to get the King to sign."[14]

Finally, on April 12, 1732, the King did sign the Charter,[15] and on June 9th it was witnessed at Westminster "by Writ of Privy Seal" and countersigned by Cocks.[16] The date June 9th was taken as the official date of issue, but the Charter did not actually pass all the necessary offices of the Government until the latter part of June. Even then some errors made in transcribing had to be amended and the document passed under the Seal again sometime during the first week in July.[17] On July 21st the Trustees petitioned the Crown to notify officially the Governor of South Carolina of the granting of the Charter, and this request was complied with on September 28th.[18]

The Charter of Georgia bore much in common with the charters of the earlier English Colonies in America, par-

---

[14] Egmont's *Diary,* I, 235.

[15] *Ibid.,* I, 260; 262. It is difficult to be certain of these dates. Compare, *e. g., The* (London) *Daily Post,* June 10, 1732, p. 1, col. 2.

[16] *America and West Indies, 1732,* p. 146.

[17] Egmont's *Diary,* I, 282-283.

[18] *Acts of Privy Council,* III, 305; *Journal, Board of Trade, 1728-1734,* pp. 313-14, 316.

ticularly the Charters of 1609 and 1612 for the first of these Colonies and the Charter of 1629 for Massachusetts Bay, albeit the Georgia Charter was a provincial charter, not one granted to a commercial company. But though a composite picture shows certain dominant features to stand out in fairly sharp relief as common to the governments of all the Colonies, no two of them were governed exactly alike. On the basis of the forms of their charters it has become customary to classify those colonies as "royal" or "crown" in which control was directly under the King; "charter" or "corporate" in which a charter was granted directly to the colony; and "proprietary" in which the grant was to a landlord or proprietor. If Georgia must be pressed under any one heading of this threefold classification, then the last is the most appropriate; but inasmuch as the term "proprietary" suggests ownership as property rather than the execution of a trust, no more inappropriate label could be chosen for Georgia, as an examination of the Charter will make clear.[19]

Regarded objectively, the Charter is a document some twenty pages in length, written in a cumbersome, legalistic style. There are no divisions into articles or sections, nor even into paragraphs, and the sentences are exceedingly long. The preamble stated in clear terms the threefold objective in establishing the Colony. In the first place, philanthropy combined with relief from domestic unemployment and support of the poor: "We are Credibly

---

[19] In their memorial to the King in connection with the surrender of the Charter, the Trustees recalled that the grant had been made to them *"not as Proprietors thereof* (italics in original) but as Trustees for granting the said Lands to such of your Majesty's indigent Subjects, and to such persecuted Foreign Protestants, as should desire to inhabit, and reside in the said Province." C. O. 5/671, p. 190.

The Charter of Georgia, says Sidney George Fisher, "differed from all the other colonial charters and constitutions, and was neither the charter of a trading company nor the constitution of a people, but a charitable trust or eleemosynary corporation." *The Evolution of the Constitution of the United States* (Philadelphia, 1897), 68. See also the characterization by A. Berridale Keith in his *Constitutional History of the First British Empire* (Oxford, 1930), 170; and by C. M. Andrews, *The Colonial Period of American History* (New Haven, 1938), IV, 372.

Informed that many of our Poor Subjects are through misfortunes and want of Employment reduced to great necessities . . . and if they had means to defray the Charge of Passage and other Expenses incident to new Settlements they would be Glad to be Settled in any of Our Provinces in America where by cultivating the lands at present waste and desolate they might . . . gain a Comfortable Subsistence for themselves and families. . . ." In the second place, an economic factor, for those unfortunate people might not only gain a comfortable subsistence for themselves and families "but also Strengthen Our Colonies and Encrease the trade, Navigation and Wealth of these our Realms." Finally, the factor of imperial defense in the sanction of the new Colony as a buffer state for South Carolina.

The Charter incorporated the Petitioners who were desirous of accomplishing these worthy ends as one body politic and corporate by the name of the *Trustees for establishing the Colony of Georgia in America.*[20] To this corporation was granted the territory lying "in that part of South Carolina in America which lies from the most Northern Stream of a River there commonly called the Savannah all along the Sea Coast to the Southward unto the most Southern Streams of a certain other great water or River called the Alatamaha and westward from the heads of the said Rivers respectively in Direct Lines to the South Seas," together with the islands within twenty leagues of the eastern coast of the said lands. The territory for an empire! But "what cared King George that the grant cut a wide swath through Florida, Louisiana, and Texas? Or that, incidentally, it included Albuquerque, Socorro, and

[20] The name Corporation for Establishing Charitable Colonies in America was suggested by the Petitioner's Memorial of December 7, 1730 *(America and West Indies, 1730,* p. 383), but there is no evidence that the petitioners ever contemplated more than one colony.

other New Mexico settlements?"[21] The Crown could grant but a seven-eighths interest in this land, however, for George Carteret, heir of one of the eight lord proprietors to whom Charles II had granted Carolina, with the 31st degree of north latitude as its southern boundary (thus including the Georgia grant), had not surrendered his rights as the other proprietors had done in 1729. But Lord Carteret had promised the Georgia petitioners as early as March, 1731, that "he would do what the King should do," and by an indenture bearing date of February 28, 1732, his interest was legally conferred.[22] This land was "to be holden of us our heirs and Successors as of our honour of Hampton Court in our County of Middlesex, in free and Comon Soccage and not in Capite," meaning simply that the Trustees should take an oath of allegiance to the King and pay an annual quit rent fixed at four shillings for every hundred acres of land which the Corporation should grant, but this payment was not to begin until after such land had been occupied for a period of ten years.[23] The "trust" for granting this land was vested in the "Trustees" and their successors forever.

The twenty-one Petitioners were named in the Charter as Trustees, but, following the precedents of the corporation under the Virginia Charters and the Company of Massachusetts Bay rather than that of the Council for New England, the membership of the Georgia Corporation might be

[21] H. E. Bolton, and M. Ross, *The Debatable Land* (Berkeley, California, 1925), 71. With all the subsequent changes in boundary, Georgia remains the largest State east of the Mississippi.

[22] Allen D. Candler, Editor, *The Colonial Records of Georgia* (Atlanta, 1904), II, 20, 152; Egmont's *Diary*, I, 155, 278, 313.

[23] Land in England in the 17th Century continued to be held under feudal terms: frankalmoin, grand serjeanty, petty serjeanty, and knight service. These old feudal tenures were not adapted to the changing civilization, however, and since 1660 they had in general been merged into the one great tenure of free and common soccage, which carried with it only the obligations of an oath, of allegiance in the case of the King, of fidelity in the case of lesser lords, and the payment of a fixed rent. This "quit rent" freed the tenant from any service, military or otherwise. Sir Frederick Pollock, *The Land Law* (London, 1896), 59, 130-131. See also Ch. IV, "The Proprietaries: Introductory," and the notes of pages 139 and 202-203 in C. M. Andrews, *The Colonial Period of American History*, II.

increased indefinitely. New members should be chosen by a two-thirds vote of the Trustees present at a yearly meeting to be held on the third Thursday in March. Both to insure the charitable aims of the Corporation and to make them clear to the public, the Trustees were prohibited from receiving any salary; and should any Trustee accept an office of profit, he should lose his membership in the Corporation. In addition, a Trustee could not hold land in Georgia, nor could land be granted to anyone in trust for his benefit. These provisions removing the possibility of gain from the Trustees were sufficient to make, as Professor Osgood has expressed it, "a radical difference between Georgia and all other proprietary provinces. . . . Whatever service was performed for the Colony by the proprietors must be disinterested and without a view to profit . . ., a condition precisely the opposite of that which lay at the base of all other proprietorships."[24]

It was laid down that the Trustees should prepare such laws as were necessary for the governance of the Colony, provided such laws be not repugnant to the statutes of England, and that they be approved by the King in Council. There were no provisions like those in the Charters of Maryland, Carolina, and Pennsylvania requiring the consent of the colonists to the laws. The only liberty specifically guaranteed to the settlers was freedom of religion, "except (to) Papists," although a blanket guarantee of the rights of Englishmen might be drawn from the provision that "all and every the persons which shall happen to be born within the said Province and every of their Children and Posterity shall have and Enjoy all Liberties Franchises and Immunities of free Denizens and natural born Subjects within any of our Dominions to all intents and purposes

[24] Herbert L. Osgood, *The American Colonies in the Eighteenth Century* (New York, 1924), III, 36-37.

as if they had been abiding and born within this our Kingdom of Great Britain or any other of our Dominions."[25]

In that it would "be too great a burden upon all the members of the said Corporation to be Convened so often as . . . (might) be requisite to hold meetings for the settling supporting Ordering and maintaining Such Colony," a smaller body of fifteen members was named in the Charter as a Common Council. After the increase in the membership of the Trustees, the number of Common Councilmen should be increased to twenty-four. Membership was to continue during good behavior, with power vested in the Common Council to fill vacancies by election from among the Trustees. It was evidently intended that this smaller body should manage the routine and ordinary business of the Corporation; yet it was vested also with "full power and authority" in numerous matters of importance: it was to apply all the monies and effects belonging to the Corporation in such manner as it should think best, enter any covenant or contract deemed advisable, appoint and remove such officers, both for the Corporation and for the government in the Colony, as were thought necessary, and fix their salaries, and lastly, to grant land to settlers, provided that no more than five hundred acres be granted to any one person. In view of the importance of these functions, the precaution was set up that no action could be taken at a meeting of less than eight Common Councilmen. As this quorum proved difficult to obtain it was fortunate that the Charter left to the Board of Trustees, with no stated quorum, many general functions, including the passing of by-laws for the Corporation, approving persons to take subscriptions, setting up courts in the Colony, and making laws for its governance.

---

[25] This provision was interpreted liberally in the contemporary press. The liberties guaranteed were said to extend to those transported to the Colony as well as those born there. See *The Political State of Great Britain*, XLIV (Aug., 1732), 151-152.

Although the Charter represented a marked departure from the prevailing policy of concentrating colonial administration in the Crown, seven provisions more rigid than had accompanied any former proprietary grant insured imperial control: *First*, and most important for the point under consideration, the authority granted to the Trustees for governing the Colony was granted for a period of twenty-one years only, after which time control would pass into the hands of the Crown; *second*, no laws, as noted above, would have force until approved by the King in Council; *third*, the governor for the Colony should be approved by the King, and should give security for observing the acts of Parliament relating to trade and navigation, and for obeying all instructions sent to him by the King in pursuance of these acts; [26] *fourth*, the Corporation should file an annual report of all receipts and expenditures with any two of several crown officers named; *fifth*, reports on the progress of the Colony should be given "from time to time" to one of the principal Secretaries of State and to the Board of Trade; *sixth*, all land grants should be carefully registered, and the Crown should receive annual reports upon these grants and should reserve the right to make special surveys if deemed necessary to ascertain the quit rents due; *seventh*, the chief command of the militia was placed in the royal governor of South Carolina. Taken as a whole these clauses provided ample authority for the Crown to see to it that the Georgia experiment did not pass beyond its control; in any case the departure from the favored colonial policy would be only temporary.

---

[26] This provision, as one might suspect, was placed in the Charter at the behest of the Board of Trade. It is interesting to note that in its report of December 30, 1730, the Board of Trade laid it down that "the person who superintends this Settlement . . . altho' he shall not act under the title of Governor should . . . not only be approved by H. M. . . . but also take the naval oath to observe the Acts of Trade and Navigation. . . ." *America and West Indies, 1730*, 396-397. In view of the fact that the Trustees never appointed a governor and of the friction arising with the Board of Trade, this wording, had it been incorporated into the Charter, would probably have taken on great significance.

In practice the Crown gave the Trustees a free hand in the management of their colonial venture. A total of seventy-one Trustees was selected during the twenty years that the Charter was in force, but of these the great majority never gave any considerable time to the project. Dr. McCain estimates that a small group of seven "had more to do with the constructive policy of the Trustees than all the other sixty-four members of the Trust combined."[27] In Egmont's own fitting words, "It is a melancholy thing to see how zeal for a good thing abates when the novelty is over, and when there is no pecuniary reward attending the service."[28]

The failure to secure further financial support from Parliament in 1751 led the Trustees to open negotiations with the Crown toward surrendering their Charter. On April 25th the Common Council appointed a committee "to adjust with the Administration the proper means for supporting and settling the Colony for the future."[29] On May 6th a memorial was presented to the Privy Council praying that sufficient funds might be appropriated to enable the Trustees to discharge the obligations already contracted. For the future, stated the Memorial, proper means should be provided "for putting the Government of the Colony on a more sure Foundation than it is at present thro' the uncertainty of the Trustees' being enabled to support it."[30] According to the procedure of the day this Memorial was referred to a Committee of the Privy Council and thence to the Board of Trade. This latter body in turn requested reports on the matter from the Admiralty, opinions from the Attorney-General, and advice from the Lords Justices. The negotiations extended over a little more than a year.[31]

[27] James Ross McCain, *Georgia as a Proprietary Province* (Boston, 1917), 39.
[28] *Diary*, III, 124.
[29] *Colonial Records of Georgia*, II, 506.
[30] C. O. 5/671, pp. 189-194; *Acts of the Privy Council*, IV, 123-124.
[31] The fullest account of these transactions is given in the *Journal of the Board of Trade, 1750-1753*, p. 197ff.

The Trustees represented the Colony as then in a flourishing way, with prospects for rapid advancement, but held the uncertainty of financial support under the present system to hazard the loss of all that had been done. In response to a query from the Board of Trade at one of the hearings as to the possibility of the inhabitants' bearing the expense of government by taxes upon themselves, "they declared it as their opinion that in their present circumstances they could not bear any burden of that sort," a view hardly in accord with the picture of the thriving condition of the Colony.[32]

Acting upon the advice of two law officers of the Crown, Ryder and Murray, the Trustees executed under their common seal a deed of surrender of all their interest in Georgia. They gave up not only their authority to govern the Colony, which by the Charter's terms would have expired on June 9, 1753, but also their trusteeship for granting the land which had been placed in the Georgia Corporation forever. The one-eighth interest in the land which the Trustees had secured from Lord Carteret was included with the rest Having closed out their business, on June 23, 1752, the last entry was made in the Trustees' records and their seal was defaced. June 25th was taken as the official date for the surrender of the Charter.[33]

---

[32] *Journal of Board of Trade, 1750-1753*, p. 213.
[33] *Acts of Privy Council*, IV, 128; *Journal of Board of Trade, 1750-1753*, p. 400.

PART II

[illegible]
Lord Viscount
& others Commission

George the Second by the Grace of God &c
To all to whom these Presents shall come
Greeting Whereas Wee are Credibly Informed that
many of our Poor Subjects are through misfortunes
and want of Employment reduced to great
necessities insomuch as by their labour they are
not able to provide a maintenance for themselves
and families and if they had means to defray
the Charges of Passage and other Expences incident
to new Settlements they would be glad to be
settled in any of our Provinces in America where by
Cultivating the lands at present waste and
desolate they might not only gain a Comfortable
Subsistance for themselves and families but also
strengthen our Colonies and encrease the trade
Navigation and Wealth of these our Realms And
Whereas our Provinces in North America have
been frequently ravaged by Indian Enemies more
Especially that of South Carolina which in the
late war by the neighbouring Savages was
laid wast with fire and Sword and great
numbers of the English Inhabitants miserably
massacred and our loving Subjects who now
Inhabit there by reason of the smallness of
their numbers will in case of any new war be
Exposed to the like Calamities in as much as
their whole Southern Frontier continueth unsettled
and lieth open to the said Savages And whereas
Wee think it highly becoming Our Crown and
royal Dignity to protect all our loving Subjects

THE CHARTER OF 1732

George the Second by the Grace of God
To all To whom these Presents shall come
Greeting Whereas wee are Credibly Informed that
many of our Poor Subjects are through misfortunes
and want of Employment reduced to great
necessities insomuch as by their labour they are
not able to provide a maintenance for themselves
and Families and if they had means to defray
the Charge of Passage and other Expenses incident
to new Settlements they would be Glad to be
Settled in any of our Provinces in America whereby
Cultivating the lands at present wast and
desolate they might not only gain a Comfortable
Subsistence for themselves and families but also
Strengthen our Colonies and Encrease the trade
Navigation and wealth of these our Realms And
whereas our Provinces in North America have
been frequently Ravaged by Indian Enemies more
Especially that of South Carolina which in the
late war by the neighbouring Savages was
laid wast with Fire and Sword and great
numbers of the English Inhabitants miserably
Massacred And our Loving Subjects who now
Inhabit these by reason of the Smallness of
their numbers will in case of any new war be
Exposed to the like Calamities in as much as
their whole Southern Frontier continueth unsettled
and lieth open to the said Savages And whereas
wee think it highly becoming Our Crown and
Royal Dignity to protect all our Loving Subjects

be they ever so distant from us to extend our
fatherly compassion even to the meanest and
most unfortunate of our people and to releive
the wants of our abovementioned poor subjects and
that it will be highly conducive for the
accomplishing those ends that a regular colony
of the said poor people be settled and established
in the southern territories of Carolina and whereas
wee have been well assured that if wee would
be graciously pleased to erect and settle a
corporation for the receiving managing and
disposing of the contributions of our loving subjects
divers persons would be induced to contribute
to the uses and purposes aforesaid know yee
therefore that wee have for the considerations
aforesaid and for the better and more orderly
carrying on the said good purposes of our
special grace certain knowledge and meer motion
willed ordained constituted and appointed and
by these presents for us our heirs and successors
do will ordain constitute declare and grant that
our right trusty and welbeloved John Lord Viscount
Percivall of our kingdom of Ireland our trusty and
welbeloved Edward Digby George Carpenter James
Oglethorpe George Heathcote Thomas Tower Robert
Moore Robert Hucks Rogers Holland William Sloper
Francis Eyles John Laroche James Vernon William
Belitha Esquires Stephen Hales Master of Arts
John Burton Batchelor in Divinity Richard Bundy
Master of Arts Arthur Bedford Master of Arts Samuel
Smith Master of Arts Adam Anderson and Thomas
Coram Gentlemen and such other persons as shall
be elected in the manner hereinafter mentioned and
their successors to be elected in manner as
hereinafter is directed be and shall be one body
politick and corporate in deed and in name by
the name of The Trustees for establishing the
Colony of Georgia in America and them and their
successors by the same name wee do by these
presents for us our heirs and successors really

be they never so distant from us to Extend our Fatherly Compassion even to the meanest and most unfortunate of our people and to relieve the wants of our abovementioned poor Subjects And that it will be highly Conducive for the accomplishing those Ends that a Regular Colony of the said poor people be Settled and Established in the Southern Frontiers of Carolina and whereas wee have been well Assured that if wee would be Graciously pleased to Erect and Settle a Corporation for the receiving managing and Disposing of the Contributions of our Loving Subjects divers persons would be Induced to Contribute to the uses and purposes aforesaid Know yee therefore that wee have for the Considerations aforesaid and for the better and more Orderly Carrying on the said good purposes of our Especial Grace certain Knowledge and Meer Motion Willed Ordained Constituted and Appointed And by these Presents for us our Heirs and Successors Do Will Ordain Constitute Declare and Grant that our Right Trusty and Wellbeloved John Lord Viscount Percival of our Kingdom of Ireland Our trusty and Wellbeloved Edward Digby George Carpenter James Oglethorpe George Heathcote Thomas Tower Robert More Robert Hucks Rogers Holland William Sloper Francis Eyles John Laroche James Vernon William Belitha Esquires Stephen Hales Master of Arts John Burton Batchelor in Divinity Richard Bundy Master of Arts Arthur Bedford Master of Arts Samuel Smith Master of Arts Adam Anderson and Thomas Coram Gentlemen and Such other persons as shall be Elected in the manner hereinafter mentioned and their Successors to be Elected in manner as hereinafter is directed be and shall be one Body Politick and Corporate in Deed and in name by the Name of The Trustees for Establishing the Colony of Georgia in America and them and their Successors by the same name wee do by these Presents for us our Heirs and Successors Really and fully make Ordein constitute and declare to be one body politick and Corporate in deed and in name for ever and that by the same name they and their Successors shall and may have perpetuall Succession and that they and their Successors by that name shall and may forever hereafter be persons able and capable in the law to purchase have take receive and enjoy to them and their Successors any mannors messuages lands Tenements rents advowsons liberties priviledges Jurisdictions ffranchises and other hereditaments whatsoever lying and being in any part of Great Brittain of whatsoever nature kind and quality they be in ffee and in perpetuity not exceeding the yearly value of One thousand pounds beyond reprises also Estates for lives and for years and all other manner of Goods Chattells and things whatsoever of what name nature quality or value soever they be for the better settling supporting and maintaining the said Colony and other uses aforesaid and to give grant lett and demise the said mannors messuages lands Tenements hereditaments Goods Chattells and things whatsoever aforesaid by lease or leases for Term of years in possession at the time of Granting thereof and not in reversion not exceeding the Term of one and thirty years from the time of Granting thereof On which in case no ffine be taken shall be reserved the full value and in case a ffine be taken shall be reserved at least a moiety of the full value that the same shall reasonably and bonafide be worth at the time of such demise and that they and their Successors by the name aforesaid shall and may for ever hereafter be persons able and capable in the law to purchase have take receive and enjoy to them and their Successors any lands Territories possessions Tenements Jurisdictions ffranchises and other hereditaments whatsoever lying and being in America of what quantity quality or value soever, and fully make Ordain Constitute and declare to be one Body politick and Corporate in Deed and in name for ever And that by the same name they and their Successors shall and may have perpetual Succession And that they and their Successors by that name shall and may forever hereafter be persons able and capable in the law to purchase have take receive and Enjoy to them and their Successors any Mannors Messuages lands Tenements Rents Advowsons liberties priviledges Jurisdictions Franchises and other hereditaments whatsoever lying and being in any part of Great Britain of whatsoever nature kind and quality they be in Fee and in Perpetuity not Exceeding the Yearly value of One thousand pounds beyond Reprises also Estates for lives and for years and all other manner of Goods Chattels and things whatsoever of what name nature quality or value soever they be for the better Settling Supporting and maintaining the said Colony and other uses aforesaid and to Give Grant Let and Demise the said Mannors Messuages Lands Tenements Hereditaments Goods Chattells and things whatsoever aforesaid by lease or leases for Term of years in possession at the time of Granting thereof and not in Reversion not Exceeding the Term of one and thirty years from the time of Granting thereof on which in case no Fine be taken shall be reserved the full value and in case a Fine be taken shall be reserved at least a Moyety of the full value that the same shall reasonably and bonafide be worth at the time of such demise And that they and their Successors by the name aforesaid shall and may for ever hereafter be persons able and capable in the law to purchase have take receive and Enjoy to them and their Successors any lands Territories possessions Tenements jurisdictions Franchises and other herditaments whatsoever lying and being in America of what quantity quality or value Soever

they be for the better settling supporting and
maintaining the said Colony And that by the name
aforesaid they shall and may be able to sue and
be sued plead and be impleaded answer and be
answered unto defend and be defended in all courts
and places whatsoever and before whatsoever judges
justices or other officers of us our heirs and
successors in all and singular actions plaints pleas
matters suits and demands of what kind nature or
quality soever they be and to act and do all
other matters and things in as ample manner
and form as any other our liege subjects of
this our realm of Great Britain and that they
and their successors forever hereafter shall and
may have a common seal to serve for the
causes and business of them and their successors
and that it shall and may be lawful for
them and their successors to change break alter
and make new the said seal from time to time
and at their pleasure as they shall think best
And we do further grant for us our heirs and
successors that the said Corporation and the
common council of the said Corporation hereinafter
by us appointed may from time to time and at
all times meet about their affairs when and where
they please and transact and carry on the business
of the said Corporation and for the better
execution of the purposes aforesaid we do by
these presents for us our heirs and successors
give and grant to the said Corporation and their
successors that they and their successors forever
may upon the third Thursday in the month of
March yearly meet at some convenient place to
be appointed by the said Corporation or the major
part of them who shall be present at any meeting
of the said Corporation to be had for the
appointing of the said place and that they or
two thirds of such of them that shall be present
shall at such yearly meeting and at no other
meeting of the said Corporation between the hours

they be for the better Settling Supporting and maintaining the said Colony And that by the name aforesaid they shall and may be able to Sue and be Sued Plead and be Impleaded Answer and be Answered unto Defend and be Defended in all Courts and places whatsoever and before whatsoever Judges Justices or other Officers of us our Heirs and Successors in all and Singular Actions Plaints Pleas matters suits and demand of what Kind nature quality Soever they Be and to Act and do all other matters and things in as ample manner and form as any other our Liege Subjects of this our Realme of Great Britain And that they and their Successors forever hereafter shall and may have a Comon Seal to serve for the Causes and business of them and their Successors And that it shall and may be lawful for them and their Successors to Change break alter and make new the said Seal from time to time and at their pleasure as they shall think best And wee do further Grant for us our Heirs and Successors that the said Corporation and the Comon Council of the said Corporation hereinafter by us appointed may from time to time and at all times meet about their Affairs when and where they please and transact and carry on the business of the said Corporation And for the better Execution of the purposes aforesaid wee do by these Presents for us our Heirs and Successors Give and Grant to the said Corporation and their Successors that they and their Successors forever may upon the third Thursday in the month of March Yearly meet at some convenient place to be appointed by the said Corporation or the Major part of them who shall be present at any meeting of the said Corporation to be had for the appointment of the said place and that they or two thirds of such of them that shall be present shall at such Yearly meeting and at no other meeting of the said Corporatdion between the hours

of them in the morning and then in the afternoon of
the same day chuse and elect such person or
persons to be members of the said corporation
as they shall think beneficial to the good designs
of the said corporation and our further will and
pleasure is that if it shall happen that any of
the persons hereafter by us appointed as the
common council of the said corporation or any
other persons to be elected and admitted members
of the said common council in the manner hereafter
directed shall die or shall by writing under his
and their hands respectively resign his or their
office or offices of common council man or
common council men the said corporation or the
major part of such of them as shall be
present shall and may at such meeting on the
said last Thursday in March yearly in manner as
aforesaid next after such death or resignation and
at no other meeting of the said corporation elect
and chuse one or more person or persons being
members of the said corporation into the room or
place of such person or persons so dead or so
resigning as to them shall seem meet and our will
and pleasure is that all and every the person or
persons which shall from time to time hereafter
be elected common council men of the said
corporation as aforesaid do and shall before he
or they act as common council men of the said
corporation take an oath for the faithful and
due execution of their office which oath the
president of the said corporation for the time
being is hereby authorized and required to administer
to such person or persons so elected as aforesaid.
And our will and pleasure is that the
first president of the said corporation shall be
our trusty and wellbeloved the said John Lord
Viscount Percival and that the said president
shall within thirty days after the passing of
this charter cause summons to be issued to
the several members of the said corporation

of Ten in the morning and four in the afternoon of the Same Day Chuse and Elect such person or persons to be members of the said Corporation as they shall think beneficial to the good Designs of the said Corporation And our further will and pleasure is that if it shall happen that any of the persons hereinafter by us appointed as the Comon Council of the said Corporation or any other persons to be Elected and admitted members of the said Comon Council in the manner Hereinafter directed shall die or shall by writing under his and their hands respectively resign his or their Office or Offices of Comon Council man or Comon Council men the said Corporation or the Major part of such of them as shall be present shall and may at such meeting on the said last Thursday in March Yearly in manner as aforesaid next after such death or Resignation and at no other meeting of the said Corporation Elect and Chuse one or more person or persons being members of the said Corporation into the Room or place of such person or persons so dead or so resigning as to them shall seem meet And Our Will and pleasure is that all and every the person or persons which shall from time to time hereafter be Elected Comon Council men of the said Corporation as aforesaid do and shall before he or they Act as Comon Council men of the said Corporation take an Oath for the Faithful and due Execution of their Office which Oath the President of the said Corporation for the time being is hereby Authorized and required to Administer to such person or persons so Elected as aforesaid And Our will and pleasure is that the First President of the said Corporation shall be our Trusty and Wellbeloved the said John Lord Viscount Percival and that the said President shall within thirty days after the passing of this Charter cause Summones to be Issued to the several members of the said Corporation them particularly named to meet at such time and place as he shall appoint to consult about and transact the business of the said Corporation. And our Will and Pleasure is And Wee Doe by these Presents for us our Heirs and Successors Ordain and Direct that the Comon Councill of the said Corporation shall consist of fifteen in number, And Wee doe by these Presents nominate Constitute and Appoint our Right Trusty and Welbeloved John Lord Viscount Percivall Our trusty and Welbeloved Edward Digby George Carpenter James Oglethorpe George Heathcote Thomas Tower Robert More Robert Hucks Rogers Holland William Sloper Francis Eyles John Laroche James Vernon William Belitha Esquires and Stephen Hales Master of Arts to be the Comon Councill of the said Corporation to continue in their said Offices during their good Behaviour And Whereas it is our Royall Intention that the members of the said Corporation should be increased by Election as soon as conveniently may be to a greater number than is hereby nominated Our further Will and Pleasure is And wee do hereby for us our Heires and Successors Ordain and Direct that from the time of such increase of the members of the said Corporation the number of the said Comon Councill shall be increased to Twenty four And that at the same Assembly at which such Additionall members of the said Corporation shall be chosen there shall likewise be Elected in the manner herein before directed for the Election of Comon Councill men nine persons to be of the said Comon Councill and to make up the number thereof twenty four And our further Will and Pleasure is that our trusty and Welbeloved the said Edward Digby Esquire shall be the first Chairman of the Comon Councill of the said Corporation And that the said Lord Viscount Percivall shall be and continue President of the said Corporation And the said Edward Digby shall be herein particularly named to meet at such time and place as he shall appoint to consult about and transact the business of the said Corporation And our will and pleasure is And wee do by these Presents for us our Heirs and Successors Grant Ordain and Direct that the Comon Council of the said Corporation shall consist of fifteen in number And wee do by these Presents Nominate Consitute and appoint Our Right Trusty and Wellbeloved John Lord Viscount Percival Our Trusty and Wellbeloved Edward Digby George Carpenter James Oglethorpe George Heathcote Thomas Tower Robert More Robert Hucks Rogers Holland William Sloper Francis Eyles John Laroche James Vernon William Belitha Esquires and Stephen Hales Master of Arts to be the Comon Council of the said Corporation to continue in their Said Offices during their good behavior and Whereas it is our Royal Intention that the members of the said Corporation should be Increased by Election as soon as Conveniently may be to a greater number than is hereby nominated Our further will and pleasure is And wee do hereby for us our Heirs and Successors Ordain and direct that from the time of Such Increase of the members of the said Corporation the number of the said Common Council shall be Increased to Twenty four And that at the same Assembly at which such Additional members of the said Corporation shall be Chosen there shall likewise be Elected in the manner thereinbefore directed for the Election of Comon Council men nine persons to be of the said Comon Council and to make up the number thereof twenty four And our further will and pleasure is that our trusty and wellbeloved the said Edward Digby Esquire shall be the First Chairman of the Comon Council of the said Corporation And that the said Lord Viscount Percival shall be and continue President of the said Corporation And the said Edward Digby shall be and continue Chayrman of the Comon Councill of the said Corporation respectively untill the meeting which shall be held next and imediately after the first meeting of the said Corporation or of the Comon Councill of the said Corporation respectively and no longer att which said second meeting and att every other subsequent and future meeting of the said Corporation or of the Comon Councill of the said Corporation respectively in order to preserve an indifferent rotation of the severall offices of President of the Corporation and of Chayrman of the Comon Councill of the said Corporation Wee do hereby ordain that all and every the person and persons members of the said Common Councill for the time being and no others being present att such meetings shall severally and respectively in their turns preside at the meetings which shall from time to time be had and held of the said Corporation or of the Common Councill of the said Corporation respectively And in case any doubt or question shall att any time arise touching or concerning the turn or right of any member of the said Comon Councill to preside att any meeting of the said Corporation or of the Comon Councill of the said Corporation the same shall be respectively determined by the major part of the said Corporation or of the Comon Councill of the said Corporation respectively who shall be present att such meeting Provided allways that no member of the said Comon Councill having served in the Office of President of the said Corporation or of Chayrman of the Comon Councill of the said Corporation shall be capable of being or of serving as President or Chayrman att any meeting of the said Corporation or of the Comon Councill of the said Corporation next and imediately ensueing that in which he so served as President of the said Corporation or Chayrman of the Comon Councill of the said Corporation respectively unless it shall soe and continue Chairman of the Comon Council of the said Corporation respectively until the meeting which shall be had next and imediately after the first meeting of the said Corporation or of the Comon Council of the said Corporation respectively and no loñger at which said Second meeting and at every other Subsequent and future meeting of the said Corporation or of the Comon Council of the said Corporation respectively in Order to preserve an Indifferent Rotation of the several Offices of President of the Corporation and of Chairman of the Comon Council of the said Corporation wee do direct and Ordain that all and every the person and persons members of the said Common Council for the – being and no others being present at such meetings shall severally and respectively in their Turns preside at the meetings which shall from time to time be had and held of the said Corporation or of the Common Council of the said Corporation respectively And in case any doubt or question shall at any time arise touching or concerning the Turn or Right of any member of the said Comon Council to preside at any meeting of the said Corporation or of the Comon Council of the said Corporation the same shall be respectively determined by the Major part of the said Corporation or of the Comon Council of the said Corporation respectively who shall be present at such meeting Provided always that no member of the said Comon Council having served in the Office of President of the said Corporation or of Chairman of the Comon Council of the said Corporation shall be capable of being or of serving as President or Chairman at any meeting of the said Corporation or of the Comon Council of the said Corporation next and imediately ensueing that in which he so Served as President of the said Corporation or Chairman of the Comon Council of the said Corporation respectively unless it shall soe

happen that at any such meeting of the said
Corporation there shall not be any other member
of the said Comon Councill present and our Will =
and pleasure is that all and every the meetings
of the said Corporation or of the Comon Councill
of the said Corporation the President or Chairman
for the time being shall have a vote and = =
shall vote and act as a Member of the said
Corporation or of the Common Councill of the = =
said Corporation at such meetings and in case of
an Equality of Votes the said President or = = =
Chairman for the time being shall have a casting
vote and our further Will and pleasure is that =
no President of the said Corporation or Chairman
of the Comon Councill of the said Corporation =
or member of the said Comon Councill or = = =
Corporation by us by these Presents appointed or
hereafter from time to time to be Elected or = =
appointed in manner as aforesaid shall have = =
take or receive directly or indirectly any Salary =
ffees perquisite benefit or profitt whatsoever for or
by reason of his or their serving the said = =
Corporation or Comon Councill of the said Corporation
as President Chairman or Comon Councill man or =
as being a Member of the said Corporation and
our Will and pleasure is that the said herein = =
before appointed President Chairman and Comon Councilmen before he and they act respectively as such =
shall severally take an Oath for the faithfull =
and due Execution of their Trust to be administred
to the President by the Cheif Baron of our = = =
Court of Exchequer for the time being and by =
the President of the said Corporation to the =
rest of the Comon Councill who are hereby = = =
authorized severally and respectively to administer =
the same and our Will and pleasure is that =
all and every person and persons who shall = =
have in his or their own name or names or = =
in the name or names of any person or persons
in trust for him or them or for his or their benefit.

happen that at any such meeting of the said Corporation there shall not be any other member of the said Comon Council present And our will and pleasure is that all and every the meetings of the said Corporation or of the Comon Council of the said Corporation the President or Chairman for the time being shall have a voice and shall vote and Act as a Member of the said Corporation or of the Common Council of the said Corporation at such meeting And in Case of an Equality of Votes the said President or Chairman for the time being shall have a Casting vote And our further will and pleasure is that no President of the said Corporation or Chairman of the Comon Council of the said Corporation or member of the said Comon Council or Corporation by us by these Presents appointed or hereafter from time to time to be Elected or appointed in manner as aforesaid shall have take or receive directly or Indirectly any Salary Fee perquisite benefit or profit whatsoever for or by reason of his or their serving the said Corporation or Comon Council of the said Corporation as President Chairman or Comon Council man or as being a member of the said Corporation And our will and pleasure is that the said herein before appointed President Chairman and Comon Council men before he and they Act respectively as such shall severally take an Oath for the Faithful and Due Execution of their Trust to be Administered to the President by the Chief Baron of our Court of Exchequer for the time being and by the President of the said Corporation to the rest of the Comon Council who are hereby Authorized Severally and respectively to Administer the same And our will and pleasure is that all and every person and persons who shall have his or their own name or names or in the name or names of any person or persons In trust for him or them or for his or their benefit

any Office place or Imployment of profit under
the Corporation shall be incapable of being
elected a member of the said Corporation and
if any member of the said Corporation during
such time as he shall continue a member thereof
shall in his own name or in the name of any
person or persons in trust for him or for his
benefit have hold exercise accept possess or enjoy
any Office place or Employment of profit under
the said Corporation or under the Common Council
of the said Corporation such member shall from
the time of such having holding exercising accepting
possessing and enjoying such Office place or
Employment of profit cease to be a member of
the said Corporation and wee doe for us our
heires and successors Grant unto the said
Corporation and their Successors that they and
their Successors or the major part of such of
them as shall be present at any meeting of
the said Corporation convened and assembled for
that purpose by proper and convenient notice
thereof shall have power from time to time and
at all times hereafter to authorize and appoint
such persons as they shall think fit to take
subscriptions and to gather and collect such moneys
as shall be by any person or persons contributed
for the purposes aforesaid and shall and may
revoke and make void such authorities and
appointments as often as they shall see cause
so to do And wee do hereby for us our heires
and successors Ordain and direct that the said
Corporation shall every year lay an account in
writing before the Chancellor or keeper or
Commissioners for the custody of the Great Seal of
Great Britain of us our heirs and successors the
Chief Justice of the Court of Kings Bench the
Master of the Rolls the Chief Justice of the Court
of Common Pleas and the Chief Baron of the
Exchequer of us our heires and successors for the
time being or any two of them of all moneys

any Office place or Imployment of profit under the Corporation shall be incapable of being Elected a Member of the said Corporation And if any member of the said Corporation during such time as he shall continue a member thereof shall in his own name or in the name of any person or persons In trust for him or for his benefit have hold Exercise accept possess or Enjoy any Office place or Employment of profit under the said Corporation or under the Comon Council of the said Corporation such Member shall from the time of such having holding Exercising accepting possessing and Enjoying such Office Place or Employment of profit cease to be a Member of the said Corporation And wee do for us our Heirs and Successors Grant unto the said Corporation and their Successors that they and their successors or the Major part of such of them as shall be present at any meeting of the said Corporation Convened and Assembled for that purpose by proper and Convenient notice thereof shall have power from time to time and at all times hereafter to Authorize and appoint such persons as they shall think fit to take Subscriptions and to gather and Collect such moneys as shall be by any person or persons Contributed for the purposes aforesaid and shall and may Revoke and make void such Authorities and appointments as often as they shall see cause so to do And wee do hereby for us our Heirs and Successors Ordain and direct that the said Corporation shall every Year lay an Account in writing before the Chancellor or Keeper or Commissioners for the Custody of the Great Seal of Great Britain of us our Heirs and Successors the Chief Justice of the Court of Kings Bench the Master of the Rolls the Chief Justice of the Court of Comon Pleas and the Chief Baron of the Exchequer of us our Heirs and Successors for the time being or any two of them of all moneys

or Effects by them received or Expended for the
carrying on the good purpose aforesaid And Wee
do hereby for us our heirs and successors Give and
Grant unto the said Corporation and their successors
full power and authority to Constitute Ordain and
make such and so many By-lawes Constitutions
Orders and Ordinances as to them or the greater
part of them at their Generall meeting for that
purpose shall seem meet necessary and convenient
for the well Ordering and Governing of the said
Corporation and the said By-lawes Constitutions
Orders and Ordinances or any of them to alter
and annull as they or the major part of them then
present shall see requisite And in and by such
By-lawes Rules Orders and Ordinances to set
Impose and Inflict reasonable pains and penalties
upon any Offender or Offenders who shall transgress
break or violate the said By-lawes Constitutions
Orders and Ordinances so made as aforesaid and
to mitigate the same as they or the major part
of them then present shall find cause which
said pains and penalties shall and may be
levyed sued for recovered retained and received
by the said Corporation and their successors or by
their Officers and Servants from time to time to
be appointed for that purpose by Action of Debt
or by any other lawfull wayes and means to the
use and behoofe of the said Corporation and
their successors All and singular which By-lawes
Constitutions Orders and Ordinances so as
aforesaid to be made Wee will shall be duly
Observed and kept under the pains and penalties
therein to be contained so alwayes as the said
By lawes Constitutions Orders and Ordinances
pains and penalties from time to time to be made
and Imposed be reasonable and not contrary or
repugnant to the lawes or Statutes of this our
Realm And that such By-lawes Constitutions and
Ordinances pains and penalties from time to time to
be made and Imposed and any repeal or alteration

or Effects by them received or Expended for the carrying on the good purposes aforsaid And wee do hereby for us our Heirs and Successors Give and Grant unto the said Corporation and their Successors full power and Authority to Constitute Ordain and make such and so many By-laws Constitutions Orders and Ordinances as to them or thė greater part of them at their General meeting for that purpose shall seem meet necessary and convenient for the Well Ordering and Governing of the said Corporation And the said By-laws Constitutions Orders and Ordinances or any of them to alter and annull as they or the Major part of them then present shall see requisite And in and by such By-laws Rules Orders and Ordinances to sett Impose and Inflict reasonable pains and penalties upon any Offender or Offenders who shall transgress break or violate the said By-laws Constitutions Orders and Ordinances so made as aforesaid and to mitigate the same as they or the Major part of them then present shall find Cause which said pains and penalties shall and may be levyed sued for taken and retained and recovered by the said Corporation and their Successors or by their Officers and Servants from time to time to be appointed for that purpose by Action of Debt or by any other Lawful Ways and means to the use and behoof of the said Corporation and their Successors all and singular Which By-laws Constitutions Orders and Ordinances so as aforesaid to be made wee will shall be duly Observed and kept under the pains and penalties therein to be contained so always as the said By laws Constitutions Orders and Ordinances pains and penalties from time to time to be made and Imposed to be reasonable and not contrary or repugnant to the laws or Statutes of this our Realm And that such By-laws Constitutions and Ordinances pains and penalties from time to time to be made and Imposed and any repeal or alteration

thereof or of any of them be likewise subject to
be Established and Confirmed by the then next meeting
of the said Corporation to be held and kept next
after the same shall be respectively made And
Whereas the said Corporation intend to settle a
Colony and to make an Habitation and Plantation
in that part of our Province of South Carolina
in America hereinafter described Know yee therefore
that Wee greatly desiring the happy Success of
the said Corporation for their further Encouragement
in accomplishing so Excellent a Work have of our
Especiall Grace certain Knowledge and meer motion
Given and Granted and by these Presents for us
our Heirs and Successors do Give and Grant to the
said Corporation and their Successors under the
Reservations Limitations and Declarations hereafter
Expressed seven undivided parts the whole into
Eight equall parts to be divided of all those
Lands Countrys and Territories Scituate lying and
being in that part of South Carolina in America
Which lies from the most Northern Stream of a
River there commonly called the Savannah all along
the Sea Coast to the Southward unto the most
Southern Stream of a certain other great Water
or River called the Alatamaha and Westward
from the Heads of the said Rivers respectively in
Direct lines to the South Seas and all that
Share Circuit and Precinct of Land lying within
the said boundaries with the Islands in the Sea
lying opposite to the Eastern Coast of the said
Lands within twenty Leagues of the same which
are not already Inhabited or Settled by any
Authority derived from the Crown of Great Britain
together with all the Soils Grounds Havens
Ports Gulfs and Bays Mines as well Royall
Mines of Gold and Silver as other Minerals
Precious Stones Quarries Woods Rivers Waters
Fishings as well Royall Fishings of Whale and
Sturgeon as other Fishings Pearls Commodities
Jurisdictions Royalties Franchises Priviledges and

thereof or of any of them be likewise agreed to be Established and Confirmed by the General meeting of the said Corporation to be held and kept next after the same shall be respectively made And whereas the said Corporation intend to settle a Colony and to make an habitation and plantation in that part of our Province of South Carolina in America hereinafter described Know yee therefore that wee greatly desiring the happy Success of the said Corporation for their further Encouragement in accomplishing so Excellent a work have of our Especial Grace certain Knowledge and Meer Motion Given and Granted And by these Presents for us our Heirs and Successors do Give and Grant to the said Corporation and their Successors under the Reservations limitations and Declarations hereafter Expressed seven undivided parts the whole into Eight equal parts to be divided of all those lands Countries and Territories Situate lying and being in that part of South Carolina in America which lies from the most Northern Stream of a River there comonly called the Savannah all along the Sea Coast to the Southward unto the most Southern Stream of a certain other great water or River called the Alatamaha and Westward from the heads of the said Rivers respectively in Direct Lines to the South Seas and all that space Circuit and Precinct of land lying within the said boundaries with the Islands in the Sea lying opposite to the Eastern Coast of the said lands within twenty leagues of the same which are not already inhabited or settled by any Authority derived from the Crown of Great Britain together with all the Soils Grounds Havens Ports Gulfs and Bays Mines as well Royal Mines of Gold and Silver as other Minerals Precious Stones Quarries Woods Rivers waters Fishings as well Royal Fishings of whale and Sturgeon as other Fishings Pearls Comodities Jurisdictions Royalties Franchises Priviledges and

preheminences within the said Territories and
the precincts thereof and thereunto in any sort
belonging or appertaining and which wee by our
letters patents may or can grant and in as
ample manner and sort as wee or any our
royall progenitors have hitherto granted to any
Company body politick or corporate or to any
Adventurer or Adventurers Undertaker or Undertakers
of any discoveries plantation or traffick of in or
unto any foreign parts whatsoever and in as
legall and ample manner as if the same were
herein particularly mentioned and expressed To
have hold possess and enjoy the said seven
undivided parts (the whole into eight equall parts
to be divided as aforesaid) of all and singular
the said lands countries and territories with all
and singular other the premisses herein before by
these presents granted or mentioned or intended to
be granted to them the said Corporation and
their successors for ever for the better support of
the said Colony to be holden of us our heirs and
successors as of our honour of Hampton Court
in our County of Middlesex in free and common
soccage and not in capite yeilding and paying
therefore to us our heirs and successors yearly
for ever the sum of four shillings for every
hundred acres of the said lands which the said
Corporation shall grant demise plant or settle the
said payment not to commence or to be made untill
ten years after such grant demise planting or
settling and to be answered and paid to us our
heirs and successors in such manner and in such
species of money or notes as shall be current
in payment by proclamation from time to time in
our said Province of South Carolina All which
lands countries territories and premisses hereby
granted or mentioned or intended to be granted
wee do by these presents make erect and create
one independent and separate Province by the
name of Georgia by which name wee will the

Prehemmences within the said Territories and the Precincts thereof and thereunto in any Sort belonging or appertaining and which wee by our letters Patents may or can grant and in as Simple manner and Sort as wee or any our Royal Progenitors have hitherto Granted to any Company Body politick or corporate or to any Adventurer or Adventurers Undertaker or Undertakers of any Discoveries Plantation or Traffick of in or unto any Foreign parts whatsoever and in as large and ample manner as if the same were herein particularly mentioned and Expressed To have hold possess and Enjoy the said Seven undivided parts the whole into Eight equal parts to be divided as aforesaid of all and Singular the said lands Countries and Territories with all and singular other the Premisses hereinbefore by these Presents Granted or mentioned or intended to be Granted to them the said Corporation and their Successors for ever for the better support of the said Colony to be holden of us our heirs and Successors as of our honour of Hampton Court in our County of Middlesex in Free and Comon Soccage and not in Capite Yeilding and paying therefore to us our heirs and Successors yearly for ever the sume of Four shillings for every Hundred acres of the said lands which the said Corporation shall Grant Demise Plant or settle the said payment not to Comence or be made until ten Years after such Grant Demise Planting or Settling and to be Answered and paid to us our Heirs and Successors in such manner and in such Species of money or Notes as shall be Current in payment by Proclamation from time to time in our said Province of South Carolina All which lands Countries Territories and Premisses hereby Granted or mentioned or intended to be Granted wee do by these Presents make Erect and Create one Independent and seperate Province by the name of Georgia by which name wee will the

same henceforth to be called and that all and
every person and persons who shall at any time
hereafter inhabit or reside within our said province
shall be and are hereby declared to be free and
shall not be subject to or be bound to obey
any laws orders statutes or constitutions which
have been heretofore made ordered or enacted or
which hereafter shall be made ordered or enacted
by for or as the laws orders statutes or constitutions
of our said province of South Carolina save and
except only the command in chief of the militia
of our said province of Georgia to our governor
for the time being of South Carolina in the
manner hereinafter declared but shall be subject to
and bound to obey such laws orders statutes and
constitutions as shall from time to time be made
ordered and enacted for the better government of
the said province of Georgia in the manner
hereinafter directed and we do hereby for us our
heirs and successors ordain will and establish
that for and during the term of one and twenty
years to commence from the date of these our
letters patent the said corporation assembled for
that purpose shall and may form and prepare
laws statutes and ordinances fit and necessary
for and concerning the government of the said
colony and not repugnant to the laws and
statutes of England and the same shall and
may present under their common seal to us our heirs
and successors in our or their privy council for our
or their approbation or disallowance and the said
laws statutes and ordinances being approved by
us our heirs or successors in our or their privy
council shall from thenceforth be in full force
and virtue within our said province of Georgia
And for as much as the good and prosperous
success of the said colony cannot but chiefly
depend next under the blessing of God and the
support of our royal authority upon the provident
and good direction of the whole enterprise and that

same henceforth to be called And that all and every person and persons who shall at any time hereafter Inhabit or reside within our said Province shall be and are hereby declared to be Free and shall not be Subject to or bound to obey any laws Orders Statutes or Constitutions which have been heretofore made Ordered or Enacted or which hereafter shall be made Ordered or Enacted by for or as the laws Orders Statutes or Constitutions of our said Province of South Carolina save and Except only the Command in Chief of the Militia of our said Province of Georgia to our Governor for the time being of South Carolina in the manner hereinafter declared but shall be Subject to and bound to obey such laws Orders Statutes and Constitutions as shall from time to time be made Ordered and Enacted for the better Government of the said Province of Georgia in the manner hereinafter directed And wee do hereby for us our Heirs and Successors Ordain Will and Establish that for and during the Term of one and twenty years to Comence from the date of these our letters Patent the said Corporation Assembled for that purpose shall and may form and prepare laws Statutes and Ordinances fit and necessary for and concerning the Government of the said Colony and not repugnant to the laws and Statutes of England and the same shall and may present under their Comon Seal to us our Heirs and Successors in our or their Privy Council for our or their Approbation or Disallowance And the said laws Statutes and Ordinances being approved by us our Heirs and Successors in our or their Privy Council shall from thenceforth be in full force and virtue within our said Province of Georgia And for as much as the Good and prosperous Success of the said Colony cannot but cheifley depend next under the blessing of God and the support of our Royal Authority upon the provident and good direction of the whole Enterprise And that in Writing to be made by them upon all the members of the said Corporation to be Convened so often as may be requisite to hold meetings for the settling supporting ordering and maintaining such Colony Therefore We do Will Ordain and Establish that the said Common Council for the time being of the said Corporation being assembled for that purpose or the major part of them shall from time to time and at all times hereafter have full power and Authority to dispose of expend and apply all the monies and effects belonging to the said Corporation in such manner and ways and in such expences as they shall think best to conduce to the carrying on and effecting the good purposes herein mentioned and intended and also shall have full power in the name and on the account of the said Corporation and with and under their Common Seale to enter into any Covenants and Contracts for carrying on and effecting the purposes aforesaid and our further will and pleasure is that the said Common Council for the time being or the major part of such of the said Common Council which shall be present and assembled for that purpose from time to time and at all times hereafter shall and may Commit Constitute and appoint a Treasurer or Treasurers Secretary or Secretaries and such other officers ministers and servants of the said Corporation as to them or the major part of such of them as shall be present shall seem proper or requisite for the good management of their affairs and at their will and pleasure to displace remove and put out such Treasurer or Treasurers Secretary or Secretaries and all such other Officers ministers or servants as often as they shall think fit so to do and others in the room Office place or station of him or them so displaced removed or put out to nominate Constitute and appoint and shall and may determine and appoint such reasonable Salaries perquisites or other it will be too great a burthen upon all the Members of the said Corporation to be Convened so often as may be requisite to hold meetings for the settling supporting Ordering and maintaining Such Colony Therefore wee do will Ordain and Establish that the said Comon Council for the time being of the said Corporation being Assembled for that purpose or the Major part of them shall from time to time and at all times hereafter have full power and Authority to dispose of Expend and apply all the monies and Effects belonging to the said Corporation in such manner and ways and in such Expences as they shall think best to Conduce to the carrying on and Effecting the good purposes herein mentioned and intended and also shall have full power in the name and on the Account of the said Corporation and with and under their Comon Seale to Enter into any Covenants and Contracts for carrying on and Effecting the purposes aforesaid And our further will and pleasure is that the said Comon Council for the time being or the Major part of such of the said Comon Council which shall be present and Assembled for that purpose from time to time and at all times hereafter shall and may Nominate Contribute and appoint a Treasurer or Treasurers Secretary or Secretarys and such other Officers Ministers and Servants of the said Corporation as to them or the Major part of such of them as shall be present shall seem proper or requisite for the good management of their Affaires and at their will and pleasure to displace remove and put out such Treasurer or Treasurers Secretary or Secretarys and all such other Officers Ministers or Servants as often as they shall think fit so to do and others in the Room Office place or Stead of him or them so Displeased removed or put out to nominate Constitute and appoint and shall and may Determine and appoint such reasonable Salaries perquisites or other

Rewards for the Labour or Service of such Officers
Servants and Persons as to the said Comon
Council shall seem meet and all such Officers
shall before they Act in their respective Offices
take an Oath to be to them Administred by the
Chairman for the time being of the said Comon
Comon Council of the said Corporation who is
hereby Authorized to Administer the same for the
faithful and due Execution of their respective Offices
and places and our Will and pleasure is that
all and every person and persons who shall from
time to time be chosen or appointed Treasurer or
Treasurers Secretary or Secretaries of the said
Corporation in manner herein before directed shall
during such time as they shall serve in the said
Offices respectively be incapable of being a member
of the said Corporation and Wee doe further of our
Especiall Grace certain knowledge and meer motion
for us our heirs and Successors Grant by these
presents to the said Corporation and their Successors
that it shall be lawfull for them and their
Officers or Agents at all times hereafter to
Transport and Convey out of our Realm of Great
Britain or any other our Dominions into the said
Province of Georgia to be there settled all such
and so many of our Loving Subjects or any
Foreigners that are willing to become our Subjects
and live under our Allegiance in the said Colony
as shall be willing to go to Inhabit and reside
there with sufficient Shipping Armour Weapons
Ordnance munition Powder Shot Victualls and such
Merchandize or Wares as are esteemed by the
Wild people in those parts Cloathing Implements
Furniture Cattle Horses Mares and all other things
necessary for the said Colony and for their use
and defence and trade with the people there and
in passing and returning to and from the same
Also Wee doe for us our heires and Successors
declare by these presents that all and every the
persons which shall happen to be born within the

Rewards for the labour or Service of such Officers Servants and persons as to the said Comon Council shall seem meet and all such Officers shall before they Sit in their respective Offices take an Oath to be to them Administered by the Chairman for the time being of the said Comon Comon Council of the said Corporation who is hereby Authorized to Administer the same for the faithful and Due Execution of their respective Offices and places And our will and pleasure is that all and every person and persons who shall from time to time be Chosen or appointed Treasurer or Treasurers Secretary or Secretarys of the said Corporation in manner hereinbefore directed shall during such time as they shall serve in the said Offices respectively be incapaable of being a member of the said Corporation And wee do further of our Especial Grace certain Knowledge and Meer Motion for us our Heirs and Successors Grant by these Presents to the said Corporation and their Successors that it shall be lawful for them and their Officers or Agents at all times hereafter to transport and Convey out of our Realm of Great Britain or any other our Dominions into the said Province of Georgia to be there settled all such and so many of our Loving Subjects or any Foreigners that are willing to become our Subjects and live under our Allegiance in the said Colony as shall willingly go to Inhabit and reside there with sufficient shipping Armour weapons Ordnance Munition Powder Shot Victuals and such Merchandize or wares as are Esteemed by the Wild people in those parts Cloathing Implements Furniture Cattle Horses Mares and all other things necessary for the said Colony and for their use and Defence and trade with the people there and in passing and returning to and from the same Also wee Do for us our Heirs and Successors declare by these Presents that all and every the persons which shall happen to be born within the

said Province and every of their children and
Posterity shall have and enjoy all liberties
franchises and Immunities of free Denizens and
naturall born Subjects within any of our Dominions
to all intents and purposes as if they had been
abiding and born within this our kingdom of
Great Britain or any other of our Dominions And for
the greater ease and encouragement of our Loving
Subjects and such others as shall come to
Inhabit in our said Colony Wee do by these
Presents for us our heirs and successors grant
establish and ordain that for ever hereafter
there shall be a liberty of conscience allowed in
the worship of God to all persons inhabiting
or which shall inhabit or be resident within
our said Province and that all such persons
except Papists shall have a free exercise of
their Religion so they be contented with the quiet
and peaceable enjoyment of the same not
giving offence or scandall to the Government And
our further will and pleasure is and Wee do
hereby for us our heirs and successors declare
and grant that it shall and may be lawfull
for the said Common Councill or the major part
of them assembled for that purpose in the name
of the Corporation and under their Common Seal
to distribute convey assign and set over such
particular portions of the lands tenements and
hereditaments by these Presents granted to the said
Corporation unto such of our loving Subjects
naturally born or Denizens or others that shall be
willing to become subjects and live under our
allegiance in the said Colony upon such terms
and for such estates and upon such rents
reservations and conditions as the same may
lawfully be granted and as to the said Common
Councill or the major part of them so present shall
seem fit and proper Provided always that no
grant shall be made of any part of the said
lands unto any person being a member of the

said Province and every of their Children and Posterity shall have and Enjoy all Liberties Franchises and Immunities of Free Denizens and natural born Subjects within any of our Dominions to all intents and purposes as if they had been abiding and born within this our Kingdom of Great Britain or any other of our Dominions And for the greater Ease and Encouragement of our Loving Subjects and such others as shall come to Inhabit in our said Colony wee do by these Presents for us our Heirs and Successors Grant Establish and Ordain that for ever hereafter there shall be a liberty of conscience allowed in the Worship of God to all persons Inhabiting or which shall Inhabit or be Resident within our said Province And that all such persons Except Papists shall have a Free Exercise of their Religion so they be contented with the quiet and peaceable Enjoyment of the Same not giving Offence or Scandal to the Government And our further will and pleasure is And wee do hereby for us our Heirs and Successors declare and Grant that it shall and may be lawful for the said Comon Council or the Major part of them Assembled for that purpose in the name of the Corporation and under their Comon Seal to Distribute Convey Assigne and Settover such particular portions of the lands Tenements and hereditaments by these Presents Granted to the said Corporation unto such of our loving Subjects Natural born or Denizens or others that shall be willing to become Subjects and live under our Allegiance in the said Colony upon such Terms and for Such Estates and upon such Rents Reservations and Conditions as the same may lawfully be Granted and as to the said Comon Council or the Major part of them so present shall seem fit and proper Provided always that no Grant shall be made of any part of the said lands unto any person being a member of the

said Corporation or to any other person in trust
for or for the benefit of any member of the
said Corporation and that no person having any
estate or interest in law or equity in any part
of the said lands shall be capable of being a
member of the said Corporation during the
continuance of such estate or interest Provided also
that no greater quantity of the said land be
granted either entirely or in parcels to or to the
use of or in trust for any one person than five
hundred acres and that all grants made contrary
to the true intent and meaning hereof shall be
absolutely null and void and we do hereby
grant and ordain that such person and persons
for the time being as shall be thereunto
appointed by the said Corporation shall and may
at all times and from time to time hereafter
have full power and authority to administer and
give the oaths appointed by an act of
Parliament made in the first year of the
reign of our late royal father to be taken
instead of the oaths of allegiance and supremacy
and also the oath of abjuration to all and every
person and persons which shall at any time be
inhabiting or residing within our said colony
and in like cases to administer the solemn
affirmation to any of the persons commonly called
Quakers in such manner as by the laws of
our realm of Great Britain the same may be
administered and we do of our further grace
certain knowledge and mere motion grant
establish and ordain for us our heirs and successors
that the said Corporation and their successors
shall have full power and authority for and
during the term of one and twenty years to
commence from the date of these our letters patent
to erect and constitute judicatures and courts of
record or other courts to be held in the name of us
our heirs and successors for the hearing and
determining of all manner of crimes offences pleas

said Corporation or to any other person In Trust for or for the benefit of any Member of the said Corporation And that no person having any Estate or Interest in law or Equity in any part of the said lands shall be capable of being a member of the said Corporation During the continuance of such Estate or Interest Provided also that no greater quantity of the said land be Granted either entirely or in parcels to or to the use of or In trust for any one person than Five Hundred Acres And that all Grants made contrary to the true intent and meaning hereof shall be absolutely null and void And we do hereby Grant and Ordain that such person and persons for the time being as shall be thereunto appointed by the said Corporation shall and may at all times and from time to time hereafter have full power and Authority to Administer and give the Oaths appointed by an Act of Parliament made in the First year of the Reign of our late Royal Father to be taken instead of the Oaths of Allegiance and Supremacy and also the Oath of Abjuration to all and every person and persons which shall at any time be Inhabiting or residing within our said Colony And in like Cases to Administer the solemn Affirmation to any of the persons comonly called Quakers in such manner as by the laws of our Realm of Great Britain the same may be Administered And wee do of our further Grace certain Knowledge and Meer Motion Grant Establish and Ordain for us our Heirs and Successors that the said Corporation and their Successors shall have full power and Authority for and during the Term of one and twenty years to Comence from the Date of these our letters Patents to Erect and Constitute jurisdictions and Courts of Record or other Courts to be held in the name of us our Heirs and Successors for the hearing and determining of all manner of Crimes Offences Pleas

Processes Plaints Actions Matters Causes and things
whatsoever arising or happening within the Province
of Georgia or between persons inhabiting or residing
there whether the same be Criminall or Civill and
whether the said Crimes be Capitall or not Capitall
and whether the said Pleas be Reall Personall or
mixed and for Awarding and making out Executions
thereupon to which Courts and Judicatures wee do
hereby for us our heirs and Successors give and
grant full power and Authority from time to
time to Administer Oaths for the discovery of
truth in any matter in Controversy or depending
before them or the Solemn Affirmation to any of
the persons commonly called Quakers in such manner
as by the Laws of our Realm of Great Britain
the same may be Administred and our further will
and pleasure is that the said Corporation and
their Successors do from time to time and at all
times hereafter Register or cause to be Registred
all such Leases Grants Plantings Conveyances
Settlements and Improvements whatsoever as shall
at any time hereafter be made by or in the
name of the said Corporation of any Lands
Tenements or Hereditaments within the said
Province and shall yearly send or transmitt or
cause to be sent and transmitted Authentick Accounts
of such Leases Grants Conveyances Settlements and
Improvements respectively unto the Auditor of the
Plantations for the time being or his Deputy and
also to our Surveyor for the time being of our
said Province of South Carolina to whom wee
do hereby grant full power and Authority from
time to time as often as need shall require to
inspect and survey such of the said Lands and
Premisses as shall be demised granted and
settled as aforesaid which said Survey and
Inspection wee do hereby declare to be intended
to ascertain the Quit Rents which shall from time
to time become due to us our heirs and
Successors according to the Reservation hereinbefore

processes Plaints Actions matters Causes and things whatsoever arising or happening within the Province of Georgia or between persons Inhabiting or residing there whether the same be Criminal or Civil And whether the said Crimes be Capital or not Capital And whether the said Pleas be Real personal or mixed and for Awarding and making out Executions thereupon to which Courts and Judicatures wee do hereby for us our Heirs and Successors Give and Grant full power and Authority from time to time to Administer Oaths for the Discovery of truth in any matter in Controversy or Depending before them or the Solemn Affirmation to any of the persons comonly called Quakers in such manner as by the laws of our Realme of Great Britain the same may be Administered And our further will and pleasure is that the said Corporation and their Successors do from time to time and at all times hereafter Register or cause to be Registered all such leases Grants Plantings Conveyances Settlements and Improvements whatsoever as shall at any time hereafter be made by or in the name of the said Corporation of any lands Tenements or hereditaments within the said Province and shall yearly send or transmit or cause to be sent and transmitted Authentick Account of such leases Grants Conveyances Settlements and Improvements respectively unto the Auditor of the Plantations for the time being or his Deputy and also to our Surveyor for the time being of our Said Province of South Carolina to whom we do hereby Grant full power and Authority from time to time as often as need shall require to inspect and Survey such of the said lands and Premisses as shall be demised Granted and settled as aforesaid which said Survey and Inspection wee do hereby Declare to be intended to Ascertain the Quit Rents which shall from time to time become due to us our Heirs and Successors according to the Reservation hereinbefore

mentioned and for no other purpose whatsoever =
hereby for us our heirs and successors strictly = =
enjoining and commanding that neither any of = =
their surveyors or any person whatsoever under the
pretext and colour of making the said surveys =
or inspection shall take demand or receive any =
gratuity fee or reward of or from any person or
persons inhabiting in the colony or from the said
corporation or common council thereof on the pain
or forfeiture of their office or offices and = = =
incurring our highest displeasure Provided always
and our further will and pleasure is that all =
leases grants and conveyances to be made by =
or in the name of the said corporation of any =
lands within the said province or a memorial =
containing the substance and effect thereof shall
be registered with the auditor of the plantations
of us our heirs and successors within the space
of one year to be computed from the date = =
thereof otherwise the same shall be void and =
our further will and pleasure is that the rents =
issues and all other profits which shall at any
time hereafter come to the said corporation = = =
issuing or arising out of or from the said = =
province or out of or from any part or parcel
of the same shall from time to time and at all
times hereafter be laid out and applied in such =
expenses and in such manner as the said common
council of the said corporation or the major part
of such of them as shall be present at any = =
meeting for that purpose assembled shall think
will most improve and enlarge the said colony
and best answer the good purposes hereinbefore
mentioned and for defraying all other charges about
the same and our will and pleasure is that the
said corporation and their successors shall from time
to time give into one of the principal secretaries =
of state and to the commissioners of trade and = =
plantation accounts of the progress of the said =
colony and our will and pleasure is that no act =

mentioned and for no other purpose whatsoever hereby for us our Heirs and Successors Strictly Enjoying and Commanding that neither our or their Surveyor or any person whatsoever under the pretext and Colour of making the said Survey or. Inspection shall take Demand or receive any Gratuity Fee or Reward of or from any person or persons Inhabiting in the said Colony or from the said Corporation or Comon Council thereof on the pain of Forfeiture of their Office or Offices and Incurring our highest Displeasure Provided always And our further will and pleasure is that all leases Grants and Conveyances to be made by or in the name of the said Corporation of any lands within the said Province or a Memorial containing the Substance and Effect thereof shall be Registered with the Auditor of the Plantations of us our Heirs and Successors within the space of one Year to be Computed from the Date thereof otherwise the same shall be void And our further will and pleasure is that the Rents Issues and all other profits which shall at any time hereafter come to the said Corporation Issuing or Arising out of or from the said Province or out of or from any part or parcel of the same shall from time to time and at all times hereafter be laid out and applied in such Expenses and in such manner as the said Comon Council of the said Corporation or the Major part of such of them as shall be present at any meeting for that purpose Assembled shall think will most Improve and Enlarge the said Colony and best Answer the good purposes hereinbefore mentioned and for Defraying all other charges about the same And our will and pleasure is that the said Corporation and their Successors shall from time to time give unto one of the Principal Secretaries of State and to the Commissioners of Trade and Plantations Accountes of the Progress of the said Colony And our will and Pleasure is that no Act

and at any meeting of the said Comon Councill
of the said Corporation shall be effectuall and
valid unless eight members at least of the said
Comon Councill including the member who shall serve
as Chairman at the said meeting be present and
the major part of them consenting thereunto And
our Will and pleasure is that the Comon Councill
of the said Corporation for the time being or
the major part of them who shall be present
being assembled for that purpose shall from time
to time for during and untill the full end and
Expiration of twenty one years to comence from
the date of these our Letters Patent have full
power and authority to nominate make constitute
Comission ordain and appoint by such name or
names stile or stiles as to them shall seem
meet and fitting all and singular such Governors
Judges Magistrates ministers and Officers civill and
military both by sea and land within the said
districts as shall by them be thought fitt and
needfull to be made or used for the Government
of the said Colony (save allways and except
such Officers only as shall by us our heirs and
Successors be from time to time constituted and
appointed for the managing collecting and receiving
such revenues as shall from time to time arise
within the said Province of Georgia and become
due to us our heirs and Successors) Provided allways
and it is our will and pleasure that every
Governor of the said Province of Georgia to be
appointed by the Comon Councill of the said
Corporation before he shall enter upon or execute
the said Office of Governor shall be allowed
and approved by us our heirs or Successors and
shall take such Oaths and shall qualify
himself in such manner in all respects as any
Governor or Comander in Chief of any of our
Colonys or Plantations in America are by law
required to do and shall give good and sufficient
Security for observing the severall Acts of Parliament

done at any meeting of the said Comon Council of the said Corporation shall be Effectual and valid unless Eight members at least of the said Comon Council including the member who shall serve as Chairman at the said meeting be present and the Major part of them consenting thereunto And our will and pleasure is that the Comon Council of the said Corporation for the time being or the Major part of them who shall be present being Assembled for that purpose shall from time to time for during and until the full End and Expiration of twenty one years to Comence from the Date of these our letters Patent have full power and Authority to nominate make Constitute Commission Ordain and appoint by such name or names Stile or Stiles as to them shall seem meet and fitting All and Singular such Governors Judges Magistrates Ministers and Officers Civil and Military both by Sea and land within the said District as shall by them be thought fit and needful to be made or used for the Government of the said Colony (save always and Except such Officers only as shall by us our Heirs and Successors be from time to time Constituted and appointed for the managing Collecting and receiving such Revenues as shall from time to time Arise within the said Province of Georgia and become due to us our Heirs and Successors) Provided always And it is our will and pleasure that every Governor of the said Province of Georgia to be appointed by the Comon Council of the said Corporation before he shall enter upon or Execute the said Office of Governor shall be allowed and approved by us our Heirs or Successors and shall take such Oaths and shall qualify himself in such manner in all respects as any Governor or Commander in Chief of any of our Colonys or Plantations in America are by law required to do and shall give good and sufficient Security for observing the several Acts of Parliament

pleasure to Rules and Instruction and to observe
and obey all Instructions that shall be sent to
him by us our heirs or successors or any Acting
under our or their Authority pursuant to the said
Acts or any of them And We do by these Presents
for us our heirs and Successors Will Grant and
Ordain that the said Corporation and their
Successors shall have full power for and during
and until the full End and Term of one and
Twenty years to commence from the date of these
our Letters Patent by any Commander or other
Officer or Officers by them for that purpose from
time to time appointed to train instruct Exercise
and govern a Militia for the Special Defence and
Safety of our said Colony to assemble in martial
Array and put in Warlike posture the Inhabitants of
the said Colony and to lead and Conduct them and
with them to encounter Expulse repel resist and
pursue by force of Arms as well by Sea as by
Land within or without the limits of our said
Colony and also to kill slay destroy and Conquer
by all fitting Ways Enterprizes and means
Whatsoever all and every person and persons as
shall at any time hereafter in an hostile manner
attempt or Enterprize the destruction Invasion detriment
or Annoyance of our said Colony and to use and
Exercise the law martial in time of actual War
Invasion or Rebellion in such Cases where by law
the same may be used or Exercised and also
from time to time to Erect Forts and Fortify any
place or places within our said Colony and the
same to furnish with all necessary Ammunition
Provision and Stores of War for Offence and
defence and to commit from time to time the
Custody and Government of the same to such
person or persons as to them shall seem meet
and the said Forts and Fortifications to
demolish at their pleasure and to take and
Surprize by all ways and means Whatsoever
all and every such person or persons with their

relating to trade and navigation and to observe and obey all Instructions that shall be sent to him by us our Heirs or Successors or any Acting under our or their Authority pursuant to the said Acts or any of them And wee do by these Presents for us our Heirs and Successors Will Grant and Ordain that the said Corporation And their Successors shall have full power for and during and until the full End and Term of one and Twenty years to Comence from the Date of these our .letters Patent by any Comander or other Officer or Officers by them for that purpose from time to time appointed to Train Instruct Exercise and Govern a Militia for the Special Defence and Safety of our said Colony to Assemble in Martial Array and put in warlike posture the Inhabitants of the said Colony and to lead and Conduct them and with them to Encounter Expulse repel resist and pursue by force of Arms as well by Sea as by land within or without the limits of our said Colony and also to kill Slay destroy and Conquer by all fitting ways Enterprizes and means whatsoever all and every such person and persons as shall at any time hereafter in an hostile manner Attempt or Enterprize the destruction Invasion Detriment or Annoyance of our said Colony and to use and Exercise the law Martial in time of Actual war Invasion or Rebellion in such Cases whereby law the same may be used or Exercised and also from time to time to Erect Forts and Fortify any place or places within our said Colony and the same to Furnish with all necessary Ammunition Provision and Stores of war for Offence and Defence and to comit from time to time the Custody and Government of the same to such person or persons as to them shall seem meet and the said Forts and Fortifications to demolish at their pleasure and to take and Surprize by all ways and means whatsoever all and every such person or persons with their

Ships Arms Ammunition and other goods as shall in
an hostile manner invade or attempt the invading
Conquering or Annoying of our said Colony And our
Will and pleasure is And Wee do hereby for us
our heirs and Successors Declare and Grant that
the Governor or Commander in Chief of the Province
of South Carolina of us our heirs and Successors
for the time being shall at all times hereafter
have the Chief Command of the Militia of our said
Province hereby Erected and Established and that such
Militia shall observe and Obey all Orders and
Directions that shall from time to time be given
or sent to them by the said Governor or Commander
in Chief any thing in these Presents before contained
to the contrary thereof in any wise notwithstanding
And of our especial ~~[illegible]~~ certain knowledge and
meer motion Wee have Given and Granted And by
these presents for us our heirs and Successors do
Give and Grant unto the said Corporation and
their Successors full power and Authority to Import
and Export their Goods at and from any port or
ports that shall be Appointed by us our heires or
Successors within the said Province of Georgia
for that purpose without being Obliged to touch
at any other Port in Carolina And Wee do by these
Presents for us our heires and Successors Will and
declare that from and after the Determination of
the said Term of one and twenty years such
Form of Government and method of making Laws
Statutes and Ordinances for the better Governing and
Ordering the said Province of Georgia and the
Inhabitants thereof shall be Established and
observed within the same as Wee our heires or
Successors shall hereafter Ordain and appoint and
shall be agreeable to Law And that from and
after the Determination of the said Term of One
and twenty years the Governor of our said
Province of Georgia and all Officers Civill and
military within the same shall from time to time
be nominated Constituted and appointed by us our

Ships Arms Ammunition and other goods as shall an hostile manner invade or attempt the invading Conquering or Annoying of our said Colony And our will and pleasure is And wee do hereby for us our Heirs and Successors Declare and Grant That the Governor or Comander in Chief of the Province of South Carolina of us our Heirs and Successors for the time being shall at all times hereafter have the Chief Comand of the Militia of our said Province hereby Erected and Established and that such Militia shall observe and Obey all Orders and Directions that shall from time to time be given or sent to them by the said Governor or Comander in Chief any thing in these Presents before contained to the contrary thereof in any wise notwithstanding And of our Especial Grace certain Knowledge and Meer Motion wee have Given and Granted And by these Presents for us our Heirs and Successors do Give and Grant unto the said Corporation and their Successors full power and Authority to Import and Export their Goods at and from any port or Ports that shall be appointed by us our Heirs or Successors within the said Province of Georgia for that purpose without being Obliged to touch at any other Port in Carolina And wee do by these Presents for us our Heirs and Successors will and declare that from and after the Determination of the said Term of one and twenty years such Form of Government and Method of making laws Statutes and Ordinances for the better Governing and Ordering the said Province of Georgia and the Inhabitants thereof shall be Established and observed within the same as wee our Heirs or Successors shall hereafter Ordain and appoint and shall be Agreeable to law And that from and after the Determination of the said Term of One and twenty years the Governor of our said Province of Georgia and all Officers Civil and Military within the same shall from time to time be nominated Constituted and appointed by us our

heirs and successors And lastly Wee do hereby for
us our heirs and successors grant unto the said
Corporation and their successors that these our letters
Patents or the Inrollment or Exemplification thereof
shall be in and by all things good firm valid
sufficient and effectual in the law according to the
true intent and meaning thereof and shall be
taken construed and adjudged in all our courts and
elsewhere in the most favourable and beneficial
sense and for the best advantage of the said
Corporation and their successors any Omission
Imperfection defect matter cause or thing whatsoever
to the contrary in any wise notwithstanding In
Witness &c Witness our self at Westminster the
ninth day of June

By Writ of Privy Seal

Heirs and Successors And lastly wee do hereby for us our Heirs and Successors Grant unto the said Corporation and their Successors that these our letters Patents or the Inrollment or Exemplification thereof shall be in and by all things good firm valid Sufficient and Effectual in the law according to the time intent and meaning thereof and shall be taken Construed and adjudged in all our Courts and elsewhere in the most favourable and beneficial sense and for the best advantage of the said Corporation and their Successors any Omission Imperfection Defect matter caüse of thing whatsoever to the contrary in any wise notwithstanding in witness as witness our self at Westminster the ninth day of June

By Writt of Privy Seal

www.ingramcontent.com/pod-product-compliance
Lightning Source LLC
Chambersburg PA
CBHW011721220426
43664CB00023B/2903
* 9 7 8 0 8 2 0 3 5 9 7 9 3 *